Contents

1 Introduction to Tax Basics

Taxable income is the foundation of your tax liability. It's the amount of your income that's subject to federal income tax. This isn't simply your gross income; various deductions and adjustments can reduce this figure. For example, contributions to a traditional IRA or health savings account (HSA) can directly lower your taxable income, resulting in a smaller tax bill. Accurately calculating your taxable income requires careful attention to detail and a thorough understanding of relevant tax laws. Seek professional advice if you're unsure about any aspect of this calculation; the cost of getting it wrong far outweighs the cost of seeking expert assistance. Remember, even seemingly small errors can lead to significant consequences. Keep detailed records of all your income and expenses to facilitate accurate tax preparation and potential future audits. Thorough record-keeping is your best defense against any potential errors or discrepancies. It is a proactive approach that showcases your commitment to accuracy and responsible tax compliance. The

IRS appreciates such diligence and it will make the process easier in case of an audit.

Your filing status significantly impacts your tax liability. Single, married filing jointly, married filing separately, qualifying widow(er), and head of household are the main categories. Your marital status on the last day of the tax year determines your filing status, unless you qualify as a surviving spouse. The choice of filing status affects your standard deduction amount, tax brackets, and eligibility for certain tax credits. For example, married couples filing jointly generally pay lower taxes than those filing separately due to the progressive nature of the tax system and the higher standard deduction. Carefully consider your individual circumstances and consult the IRS guidelines to determine the most advantageous filing status for your situation. Choosing the right status isn't just about the lowest tax; it is also about eligibility for other credits and deductions. Don't hesitate to seek professional help to make sure you are using the right status.

Understanding the difference between deductions and credits is crucial. Deductions reduce your taxable income, while credits directly reduce your tax liability. A $1,000 deduction saves you the amount of tax you would have paid on that $1,000, depending on your tax bracket. A $1,000 credit, however, directly subtracts $1,000 from your tax owed, offering a potentially greater tax savings, especially for those in higher tax brackets. This is why it's beneficial to maximize both deductions and credits whenever possible. However, remember that eligibility requirements vary for each, and careful planning is necessary to claim them accurately. The IRS has a wealth of online resources to aid you in this process, or consider enlisting the help of a tax professional for more complex situations.

Many resources are available to help you navigate the tax system. The IRS website provides comprehensive information, including publications, forms, and instructions. Tax software programs can simplify the process, guiding you through the steps and performing calculations. However, remember that these tools are only as good as the data you input. Accurately recording all your income and expenses is paramount, regardless of which method you use to file your return. Also, consider the advice of tax professionals, particularly for more complex tax situations involving business income, investments, or multiple sources of income. They can offer valuable guidance, help you to make sure you are taking advantage of all applicable deductions and credits, and ensure compliance with tax regulations.

Proper record-keeping is not just a good idea; it is essential for accurate tax preparation. Maintain detailed records of all income sources, deductions, and credits for at least three years. The IRS might audit your tax returns within this period, so meticulous records are your best protection against potential penalties or corrections. Organize your documentation in a way that's easy to access and understand. Many taxpayers find that digital storage is helpful, allowing for quick searching and easy organization. Regardless of your chosen method, ensure your records are securely stored and easily retrievable.

Finally, don't be afraid to seek professional assistance. Certified Public Accountants (CPAs) and Enrolled Agents (EAs) are qualified tax professionals who can provide guidance and support. Their expertise can be invaluable, especially for more intricate tax situations involving businesses, investments, or complex family structures. While the cost of professional help might seem significant upfront, it's often a wise investment that ensures tax compliance and minimizes the risk of costly errors. Consider it an insurance policy against potentially larger financial penalties down the line. Remember, a proactive approach to tax planning often results in significant long-term savings.

1.1 Understanding Taxable Income

Your gross income, the total amount you earned before any deductions, isn't the figure the IRS uses to calculate your tax. Instead, they focus on your taxable income, a much smaller number representing your income after eligible deductions and adjustments. Understanding this distinction is fundamental to effective tax planning, allowing you to legally minimize your tax burden and keep more of your hard-earned money.

Calculating your taxable income is a multi-step process. First, you'll start with your gross income, which encompasses wages, salaries, tips, interest, dividends, capital gains, rental income, and various other sources of income. Then, subtract above-the-line deductions. These are deductions that reduce your gross income before determining your adjusted gross income (AGI).

Examples include contributions to traditional IRAs, student loan interest payments, and health savings account (HSA) contributions. These deductions are often overlooked, but they can make a significant difference in your overall tax liability. Don't forget to meticulously document these deductions with the necessary paperwork, as the IRS requires proof for all deductions claimed. Adjusted Gross Income (AGI) is your gross income less above-the-line deductions; it serves as a crucial stepping stone in the taxable income calculation. It's a critical number because many tax deductions and credits are based on your AGI, not your gross income. For instance, eligibility for certain deductions, like the medical expense deduction, often depends on your AGI being below a specific threshold. Understanding your AGI is vital for determining whether you qualify for certain tax benefits. Always keep accurate records, because correctly calculating your AGI is essential to ensure you're taking advantage of all applicable tax breaks.

Next, you'll consider below-the-line deductions. These reduce your taxable income after you've calculated your AGI. The most significant below-the-line deductions are the standard deduction and itemized deductions. The standard deduction is a fixed amount determined by your filing status, age, and whether you are blind. It simplifies the process by providing a predetermined deduction without requiring extensive record-keeping. Itemized deductions, on the other hand, require more detailed record-keeping, but they can potentially provide larger deductions if your eligible expenses exceed the standard deduction amount.

Careful consideration of which approach–standard deduction or itemization–will minimize your tax liability is a crucial aspect of efficient tax planning. It's not a one-size-fits-all situation; you'll need to analyze your specific financial circumstances to determine the optimal strategy.

After deducting either the standard deduction or itemized deductions (whichever yields a lower taxable income), you'll arrive at your taxable income. This final figure is what the IRS uses to determine your tax liability. Remember, tax laws change frequently, so always consult the most up-to-date IRS publications and seek professional advice when needed. There is value in consulting with a tax professional, especially when facing complex financial situations or unfamiliar tax laws. They can provide personalized guidance and help navigate the complexities of the tax code to ensure you're making informed decisions that minimize your tax liability.

Many factors can affect your taxable income. Your filing status–single, married filing jointly, married filing separately, head of household, or qualifying surviving spouse– significantly impacts both the standard deduction amount and eligibility for various tax credits. Your age also plays a role, as those over 65 or who are blind are eligible for higher standard deductions. Even dependents can influence your taxable income, either through claimed exemptions or through qualifying for various tax credits like the Child Tax Credit. Understanding these factors is crucial for accurate calculation and for taking advantage of available tax benefits. Consider seeking professional guidance if you're unsure of how your specific circumstances influence your taxable income calculation.

Finally, remember that accuracy is paramount. Maintain meticulous records of all your income and expenses. Organize your financial documents systematically to streamline the tax preparation process. Accurate record-keeping protects you from potential audits and ensures that you receive all the tax benefits you're entitled to. This diligent record-keeping will ultimately save you time, money, and reduce your stress during tax season. Don't underestimate the importance of keeping organized, accurate financial records–it's the cornerstone of successful tax planning. With careful planning and accurate record-keeping, you can effectively manage your taxable income and keep more of your money.

1.2 Filing Status Overview

Your filing status significantly impacts your tax liability. Choosing the correct one is crucial for accurate tax calculations and avoiding potential penalties. It's not just about your marital status; other factors, like dependency status and residency, come into play. Understanding these nuances is essential for navigating the tax system effectively.

Single filers, as the name suggests, are unmarried individuals and not qualifying as a surviving spouse. This is a straightforward status, but it's important to confirm you don't qualify for another status that might offer a lower tax liability. Always double-check to make sure you're claiming the most advantageous status for your particular circumstances.

Married filing jointly is a status available to married couples. This option allows couples to combine their incomes and deductions, often resulting in a lower overall tax liability than filing separately. However, it also means you are jointly responsible for any tax owed. Before selecting this option, carefully assess your combined income and tax bracket.

Married filing separately is chosen by married couples who wish to keep their finances distinct. This might be due to various reasons, including specific tax circumstances or financial strategies. It's important to note that this often leads to a higher tax bill compared to filing jointly, as the tax rates are often less favorable for this filing status.

Head of household status is for unmarried individuals who maintain a household for a qualifying child or dependent relative. This status provides a more favorable tax rate than single filing but requires fulfilling specific dependency requirements and maintaining a home for the qualifying person for more than half the year. Make sure you meet all the requirements before selecting this status.

Qualifying surviving spouse is a special status available to surviving spouses for two years after the death of their spouse. This status allows them to use the married filing jointly rates, offering considerable tax advantages. This is a temporary status, so be aware of the two-year limitation and plan accordingly for future years after the period expires.

Choosing the right filing status isn't a one-size-fits-all decision. Your personal circumstances, family structure, and financial situation all influence the best choice. Don't hesitate to consult a tax professional if you need clarification. They can help you navigate the complexities and ensure you select the most beneficial status for your specific situation. Misfiling can lead to unnecessary tax burdens, so accuracy is paramount.

Remember, these descriptions are for general informational purposes and may not cover every specific nuance. Tax laws are constantly evolving, and each individual's situation is unique. Always consult official IRS guidelines and publications or seek personalized advice from a qualified tax advisor. It is better to be cautious than to incur unnecessary tax complications.

The importance of accuracy cannot be overstated. Using the wrong filing status, even unintentionally, can result in significant penalties and back taxes. Take the time to carefully gather the necessary information about your personal and financial situation before deciding on your filing status. Don't rush this crucial decision.

Proper record-keeping is essential. Keep accurate records of your income, deductions, and other relevant financial information throughout the year. This will make the process of determining your filing status and preparing your tax return much smoother and significantly reduce the risk of errors. Organize your documents meticulously.

Beyond just the initial filing, your filing status can impact your future tax planning. Your chosen status this year may influence your tax strategy in subsequent years, so understanding its long-term implications is important. Think beyond the current tax year and consider the broader picture of your financial future. This requires careful planning and possibly professional guidance.

While the IRS provides guidance on determining your filing status, it's advisable to seek professional assistance if you encounter any uncertainties or complex situations. Tax laws are complex, and a tax professional can provide personalized advice based on your unique circumstances, ensuring compliance and tax optimization. This investment in professional help can often save you far more in the long run.

2 Itemized Deductions Deep Dive

Medical expense deductions can significantly reduce your tax burden, but understanding the rules is crucial. Only expenses exceeding 7.5% of your adjusted gross income (AGI) are deductible. Keep detailed records—receipts, explanation of benefits (EOBs), and any other documentation—for all medical expenses. This includes doctor visits, hospital stays, prescription drugs, and even some transportation costs related to medical care. Remember to include expenses for yourself, your spouse, and your dependents. Don't forget about dental and vision care; they often qualify as well. Accurate record-keeping is paramount in case of an IRS audit. Organize your records chronologically and by category for efficient review and submission if necessary. Consult with a tax professional if you have complex medical situations or are unsure about the deductibility of a particular expense.

Charitable contributions are another avenue for reducing your taxable income. However, not all contributions are created equal. To be deductible, contributions must be made to qualified charities, as defined by the IRS. These typically include non-profit organizations, churches, and certain educational institutions. You can deduct cash contributions up to 60% of your AGI. For non-cash contributions like clothing or furniture, the deduction is limited to the fair market value of the item at the time of donation, and you'll need to obtain a written acknowledgment from the charity. Always obtain a receipt or acknowledgement from the organization for any donation, regardless of the amount. Keeping meticulous records is crucial for substantiating your deductions, especially for larger donations. Don't underestimate the power of donating appreciated securities; it can yield tax advantages beyond the charitable deduction itself, potentially saving you even more on taxes. It's essential to consult tax professionals to help you maximize your charitable contribution deductions and comply fully with IRS requirements.

The home office deduction can be a valuable tax break for self-employed individuals and those who have a dedicated workspace in their home used exclusively and regularly for business. The IRS requires the space to be your principal place of business or used exclusively and regularly for business, meaning it's where you conduct your administrative or management activities. The deduction can be calculated using either the simplified method or the regular method. The simplified method is easier, allowing you to deduct $5 per square foot of your home office, up to a maximum of 300 square feet. The regular method is more complex, requiring a detailed calculation based on the percentage of your home used for business. This includes calculating the square footage of your home office relative to the total square footage of your home, as well as allocating expenses such as utilities, mortgage interest, and property taxes based on this percentage. Careful record-keeping is essential, and you need to maintain detailed records of all expenses associated with your home office. Consult a tax professional to determine which method is most beneficial for your situation. Ensure you understand all requirements to avoid an audit and potential penalties. Properly utilizing this deduction can lower your tax liability considerably. Moreover, always prioritize accuracy and careful documentation to ensure compliance and avoid issues during tax season. Remember, staying organized and seeking professional guidance when needed are key factors in successfully maximizing your tax deductions.

2.1 Medical Expense Deductions

Many taxpayers overlook the potential savings offered by medical expense deductions. Understanding the rules surrounding these deductions is crucial for maximizing your tax refund or minimizing your tax liability. The IRS allows you to deduct medical expenses that exceed 7.5% of your adjusted gross income (AGI). This means you only deduct the amount surpassing that threshold. Keep meticulous records; documentation is key to successfully claiming this deduction. This includes receipts for doctor visits, hospital stays, prescription medications, and even some over-the-counter medications if prescribed by a doctor.

Don't forget about less obvious medical expenses. These can include things like transportation costs to and from medical appointments, costs associated with medical equipment such as wheelchairs or oxygen tanks, the cost of qualified long-term care, and even certain types of home modifications designed to improve accessibility for individuals with disabilities. Remember to gather all relevant documentation for each expense to support your claim. The more organized your records, the smoother the process will be.

Capital expenses related to medical care can also be deductible. This is particularly relevant if you had major medical expenses. Consider that, for example, the purchase of a wheelchair, a home elevator, or other medical equipment that would qualify as a capital expense will be depreciated. There are special rules involved in the depreciation of capital expenses, and the best approach is to consult with a tax professional to get the best advice in these situations, avoiding future problems.

While the deduction applies to expenses incurred for yourself, your spouse, and your dependents, it's essential to maintain separate records for each individual. This makes it easier during tax season and simplifies the process when filing. Furthermore, it is important to understand the rules pertaining to dependents. Only those who meet the IRS criteria for qualifying relatives or qualifying children would qualify for medical expense deduction, remember that.

Certain types of insurance premiums might also be deductible medical expenses. This includes premiums for health insurance, long-term care insurance and Medicare supplemental insurance, but not all premiums qualify. Be sure to check the IRS guidelines to confirm the deductibility of the premium you've paid, as some may not meet the criteria for a deduction. If you are unsure, seek advice from a tax professional.

The process of claiming medical expense deductions involves careful record-keeping and accurate calculations. Start by gathering all your receipts and statements for medical expenses throughout the year. Organize them chronologically or by type of expense, making it easier to calculate your total eligible expenses. Don't underestimate the power of a well-organized record-keeping system – a dedicated folder or software specifically designed for tax documentation could prove invaluable.

After totaling your medical expenses, determine your adjusted gross income (AGI). This crucial figure is used to calculate the 7.5% threshold. Subtract 7.5% of your AGI from your total medical expenses. This result represents the amount you can deduct. Remember to include only those medical expenses that are eligible for deduction according to the IRS guidelines. If your expenses don't exceed 7.5% of your AGI, you won't be able to deduct them.

When you file your taxes, use Schedule A (Form 1040), Itemized Deductions, to report your medical expense deduction. Accurately fill out the necessary sections, providing all required details about your medical expenses. Double-check all your calculations to ensure accuracy. Remember, errors on your tax return could lead to delays or even penalties. Accuracy is paramount; any doubts should be addressed by consulting with a qualified tax professional who can help you fully utilize all available deductions.

Remember, tax laws are complex and subject to change. The information provided here is for general guidance only and doesn't constitute professional tax advice. Consult with a qualified tax advisor or financial planner before making any tax decisions to ensure you take advantage of all the possible deductions and credits available to you. Always keep abreast of current IRS guidelines and updates to stay informed about any potential changes or adjustments to the rules regarding medical expense deductions. It is always better to be informed and prepared.

The IRS offers various resources to help you navigate the complexities of medical expense deductions. Their website provides comprehensive information, forms, and publications. Don't hesitate to utilize these tools to gain a better understanding of the rules and regulations. Understanding the guidelines thoroughly can reduce the risk of errors and ensure you accurately claim the deductions to which you're entitled. This thorough understanding ensures a smoother tax filing experience.

2.2 Charitable Contribution Deductions

Donating to qualified charities can significantly reduce your tax burden. However, understanding the rules surrounding charitable contribution deductions is crucial. It's not simply a matter of writing a check; specific requirements must be met to claim these deductions. Knowing the intricacies of these rules can save you considerable money.

The first thing to consider is the type of contribution you're making. Cash donations, typically the simplest to track, are generally deductible up to 60% of your adjusted gross income (AGI) for most taxpayers. This limit rises to 50% for contributions to private nonoperating foundations and supporting organizations, along with contributions of appreciated stock that don't qualify for the higher 60% limit. Remember that these are general guidelines, and specific limitations can apply depending on the charitable organization and type of contribution. Always verify directly with the organization or consult with a tax professional.

Non-cash contributions, such as donating clothing or used goods, are handled differently. You can deduct the fair market value of these items, but the deduction is limited to what a similar item would fetch at a thrift store or a used goods store, not the original purchase price. Substantiation is key; keep records of your donations, including a description of the item, its condition, and a reasonable estimate of its fair market value. For donations of items worth more than $500, it's highly recommended to obtain a written acknowledgement from the charity confirming your donation. Failing to adequately document your charitable contributions can result in your deduction being disallowed, negating the intended tax benefit entirely.

Property donations–like donating land or buildings to a charity—have unique rules. The deduction is generally based on the fair market value of the property, although there may be some adjustments depending on the use of the donated property and the nature of the organization receiving it. This valuation can be complex and often requires professional appraisal. The deduction for property is subject to various limits; for example, the amount may be limited based on your AGI. This can get especially tricky with donations that carry appreciated values. For instance, donating securities with appreciated value carries its own set of rules, which are different from other assets.

Another critical aspect is record-keeping. For cash contributions of $250 or more, you'll need a written acknowledgement from the charity, showing the amount of your contribution and the date it was made. Failure to obtain this written statement can seriously hinder your ability to deduct this specific contribution. This is also true for non-cash donations where there's a more stringent requirement for substantiation, making detailed record-keeping absolutely vital. Careful documentation is your best defense should your return ever be subject to an audit. Keeping a detailed record of your donations helps prevent future misunderstandings and potential challenges to your deduction. I strongly advise organizing these records meticulously, especially if you are involved in philanthropic activities regularly.

Furthermore, consider consulting with a tax professional. While this chapter provides a general overview, tax laws are intricate and can be interpreted differently based on individual circumstances and the nuances of certain donations. A qualified professional can help you navigate these complexities, ensuring you correctly claim all eligible deductions and avoid potential penalties. Their expertise will be invaluable in maximizing your tax savings through charitable contributions while maintaining compliance with current tax regulations. Taking this extra step helps you avoid potentially costly mistakes later.

Finally, remember that the tax benefits of charitable giving are not just about the immediate reduction in your tax liability. It's also about supporting worthwhile causes and contributing to the community. By understanding the intricacies of charitable contribution deductions, you can enhance both your personal financial well-being and the well-being of the organizations you support, making your contributions more impactful and tax-effective. Proper planning enables you to both give generously and benefit from tax advantages designed to encourage charitable activity. By carefully planning and documenting each contribution, you will maximize your tax benefits while fully supporting the causes close to your heart.

2.3 Home Office Deduction

Working from home has become increasingly common, and for many, it's a significant part of their professional lives. If you're one of them, you might be eligible for the home office deduction, a valuable tax break that can significantly reduce your tax burden. This deduction allows you to deduct a portion of your home expenses, such as mortgage interest, rent, utilities, and repairs, based on the percentage of your home used exclusively and regularly for business. Careful planning and record-keeping are vital to maximizing this deduction.

It's crucial to meet the IRS's specific requirements to claim this deduction. Your home office space must be used exclusively and regularly for business. This means it can't be used for personal purposes unless those purposes are minimal and incidental to business use. If you share your home office with family members, ensure their personal use doesn't exceed a very small percentage. For example, using it occasionally for personal emails or paying bills won't necessarily disqualify you. However, consistently using it as a guest room or children's play area would. The IRS scrutinizes this aspect of the home office deduction, therefore maintaining meticulous records is essential.

Determining the size of your home office and calculating the percentage of your home dedicated to business are vital steps. Measure your home office space accurately and compare it to the total square footage of your home. For instance, if your office occupies 100 square feet in a 1000-square-foot home, you'll use 10% (100/1000) as your business percentage for calculating your deductible expenses. Remember, this percentage applies to all eligible home expenses, ensuring the deduction accurately reflects your business's proportionate use of the home. Inconsistencies in measurements or calculations can lead to audits and potential penalties. Accurate calculations are non-negotiable.

Not all home expenses are deductible. While mortgage interest, rent, utilities, repairs, and depreciation are generally included, other expenses might not qualify. For instance, landscaping is generally not deductible, even if it improves your home office area's appearance and enhances your business operations' overall environment. Similarly, home security systems usually fall outside of deductible expenses. You must also differentiate between expenses related directly to your business and personal home maintenance costs. It's advisable to consult the latest IRS publications to stay abreast of allowable and disallowed deductions. Clarifying these differences is crucial for successful claims.

Maintaining organized records is paramount. Keep detailed records of all eligible home expenses, including receipts, bills, and canceled checks. This documentation will help you accurately calculate your deduction and successfully support your claim should the IRS request it. Develop a system for tracking expenses—digital or manual—to ensure no expenses go unrecorded. A well-organized system minimizes errors and allows for quick access to the necessary information. Consider using spreadsheet software for easy expense tracking and calculation, but always keep physical copies of supporting documents.

The simplified method, an alternative to the regular method, may be more suitable for some taxpayers. This method simplifies the calculation, allowing a deduction of $5 per square foot of your home office, up to a maximum of 300 square feet. However, this method doesn't cover all the costs that are permissible under the regular method. The simplified method is less precise but offers greater simplicity. Choosing the right method is essential for maximizing your tax savings. Carefully evaluate both the regular and simplified methods before deciding which one best suits your situation.

The home office deduction can be a significant tax benefit for those who qualify. However, it's essential to understand the IRS guidelines and maintain meticulous records to avoid penalties. Failure to maintain detailed records can result in rejection of the deduction and potentially severe financial penalties. Always ensure your records are clear, accurate, and complete, providing supporting documentation for each claimed expense. It is advisable to seek professional help from a tax advisor if you're uncertain about the eligibility requirements or calculation procedures.

Accurate calculation and proper documentation are key to successfully claiming the home office deduction. Don't underestimate the importance of carefully following the IRS guidelines; otherwise, you risk losing the opportunity for a significant tax reduction. Remember, the IRS regularly audits taxpayers claiming this deduction. Therefore, be thorough, organized, and meticulous in all aspects of your claim. By being proactive and accurate, you can increase your chances of successfully obtaining this essential deduction. Remember to seek professional help when needed; your tax advisor can guide you accurately through the process.

While the home office deduction offers a substantial tax advantage, it requires diligent effort to prepare. Thorough record-keeping, accurate calculations, and clear understanding of the eligibility criteria are all essential elements of a successful claim. This dedication minimizes potential risks and ensures that you maximize the financial benefit. The deduction can significantly impact your tax liability, making a considerable difference in your net income. Therefore, every effort toward compliance should be made with precision.

Finally, remember to review your tax situation annually and seek professional tax advice. Tax laws change, and understanding the latest updates is vital to optimizing your deductions. A qualified tax professional can offer personalized guidance tailored to your specific circumstances and help you navigate the complexities of the home office deduction. Regular review and professional guidance ensures you're always compliant and maximizing potential tax savings. Never hesitate to consult professionals when facing uncertainty.

3 Standard Deduction Strategies

The standard deduction simplifies tax filing for many. It's a fixed amount, determined annually by the IRS, that you can subtract from your gross income before calculating your taxable income. This significantly reduces the complexity of itemizing deductions, especially beneficial for those with fewer itemizable expenses. Understanding your eligibility and accurately calculating this deduction is crucial for minimizing your tax liability. For most, claiming the standard deduction is straightforward. However, specific circumstances–such as age and filing status–can affect the final amount. For instance, those aged 65 or older or who are legally blind qualify for an additional standard deduction amount. This higher deduction reflects the increased expenses often associated with aging or disability. Similarly, filing status–single, married filing jointly, head of household, qualifying widow(er)–directly impacts the standard deduction amount. The IRS publishes these specific amounts annually, so it's essential to consult the latest guidelines for the most accurate calculation.

Determining your filing status isn't always obvious. It hinges on factors like marital status, dependents, and living arrangements. For example, a single individual with no dependents will file as single, while a married couple filing jointly will use that status. Head of household status caters to unmarried individuals providing a home for a qualifying dependent. Carefully reviewing IRS guidelines ensures you choose the correct status, impacting both your standard deduction and other tax benefits. Incorrect filing status can lead to unnecessary taxes or missed deductions.

Let's clarify the interplay between itemized deductions and the standard deduction. You choose the option that results in the lower taxable income–the larger deduction, effectively. If the total of your itemized deductions exceeds the standard deduction, itemizing is advantageous. However, if the standard deduction is higher, then using that is the more tax-efficient approach. This decision-making process might require adding up all potential itemized deductions and comparing it with the standard deduction amount available to you. Tax software can greatly simplify this comparison.

Beyond the basic calculations, planning for your standard deduction can be proactive. While the standard deduction amount is set annually, understanding how life events might affect your eligibility or your filing status is crucial. For instance, marriage alters your filing status, potentially increasing your standard deduction. Similarly, reaching age 65 or experiencing a qualifying change in your living situation may also alter your eligibility for additional deductions. Anticipating these life changes, and their potential impact on your tax return, is a powerful planning tool.

A common misconception surrounds the standard deduction and dependents. While dependents do not directly increase your standard deduction, their presence might influence your filing status, indirectly affecting the amount. For example, supporting a qualifying child might allow you to file as head of household, resulting in a higher standard deduction than filing as single. This indirect relationship underscores the importance of understanding all aspects of your tax situation—the interplay between dependents, filing status, and deduction amounts.

To streamline the process, utilize available resources. IRS publications provide comprehensive details on standard deductions and filing statuses. Tax software, while often paid, frequently simplifies the calculation process, ensuring accuracy. Even free online tax filing resources can offer valuable guidance, especially for straightforward situations. Consulting a tax professional is advisable for those with complex tax scenarios. Whether using professional assistance or self-preparation, accurate record-keeping remains essential. Keep all supporting documents to justify your deductions and filing status should an IRS audit occur.

Finally, remember the standard deduction isn't static. It's adjusted annually for inflation, meaning the amount changes each year. The amount is not a fixed value; always use the updated amount available on the IRS website or through reputable tax software. Staying informed about these annual adjustments ensures you claim the maximum permissible deduction. Staying updated on these yearly changes makes a difference over time. Your proactive approach minimizes your overall tax burden, and enhances your financial well-being.

3.1 Who Qualifies?

Everyone's situation is unique, making it crucial to understand who's eligible for the standard deduction. It's a crucial starting point for efficient tax planning, a simpler alternative to itemizing deductions. The standard deduction offers a fixed amount you can subtract from your gross income, potentially lowering your taxable income and therefore your tax bill.

The amount you can deduct depends entirely on your filing status and age. For example, single filers may have a different standard deduction amount than those who are married filing jointly. Similarly, those aged 65 or older, or who are blind, receive an additional standard deduction amount. This means a married couple, both over 65, will have a significantly higher standard deduction than a young single individual. These differences highlight the personalized nature of tax planning. The IRS publishes these amounts annually, so it's essential to consult the most up-to-date information.

Understanding your filing status is paramount. Are you single, married filing jointly, married filing separately, head of household, or qualifying surviving spouse? Each status dictates the specific standard deduction amount you're entitled to claim. This is especially important because your filing status can dramatically alter your overall tax liability, even influencing your eligibility for other credits or deductions. Incorrectly choosing your filing status could lead to overpaying your taxes or even facing penalties. So, pay close attention to the IRS guidelines on this matter. Accurate filing is key.

Beyond age and marital status, other factors might affect your eligibility. For instance, are you claimed as a dependent on someone else's return? If so, your standard deduction amount will be limited, potentially leading to different tax implications than someone not claimed as a dependent. This is a crucial detail often overlooked by those unfamiliar with the complexities of tax law. It's always best to check with a tax professional if you're uncertain about your dependent status and its impact on your taxes. Remember, precise understanding is always better than guesswork.

Furthermore, certain life events can impact your standard deduction eligibility. A significant life change, such as marriage or divorce, directly alters your filing status and, consequently, your standard deduction amount. These events may trigger a change in your tax bracket and overall liability. For example, a recent marriage may enable you to file jointly, resulting in a higher standard deduction. Similarly, a divorce will require a change to your filing status and thus recalculation of the deduction. Staying informed about these changes is paramount.

It is worth mentioning that while the standard deduction simplifies the tax process for many, it might not always be the most advantageous option. Individuals with substantial itemized deductions, such as significant medical expenses or charitable contributions, may discover that itemizing results in a lower overall tax liability. This is why carefully comparing the total of your itemized deductions with the standard deduction amount is essential. A straightforward calculation can reveal which method benefits you most and allows for a more strategic approach to tax planning. This is where proper record-keeping plays a crucial role.

Let's consider a practical example. Suppose John, a 67-year-old single filer, is considering his tax options. Knowing his age and filing status, he can readily determine his standard deduction amount using the current IRS guidelines. He can then compare this figure to the sum of his itemized deductions. If his itemized deductions exceed the standard deduction, itemizing will be the more advantageous strategy for lowering his tax liability. This simple comparison underscores the importance of understanding the standard deduction as a starting point in your tax planning journey. Thorough examination can often reveal the most beneficial approach.

This underscores the necessity of accurate record-keeping throughout the year. Maintaining meticulous records of all potential deductions, such as charitable donations or medical expenses, is crucial for determining whether itemizing or taking the standard deduction is more beneficial. Efficient record-keeping isn't just about compliance; it significantly impacts your tax strategy. It ensures you have the necessary information to make informed decisions come tax season. You should keep accurate records of your income and expenses throughout the year. This makes tax preparation smoother and less stressful. Finally, don't hesitate to seek professional assistance. A tax advisor can help you navigate the complexities of tax laws and identify the most advantageous strategies for your specific situation. They will use their knowledge to determine whether the standard deduction or itemizing will result in a lower tax bill. Even seemingly straightforward situations can benefit from professional guidance, ultimately saving you time, money, and stress. Don't underestimate the value of expert advice. Professional help ensures you maximize your deductions and credits correctly.

3.2 Calculating Your Deduction

The standard deduction simplifies tax preparation; it's a flat amount you subtract from your gross income before calculating your tax. This contrasts with itemizing, where you list individual deductions. Your standard deduction amount hinges on your filing status, whether you're single, married filing jointly, married filing separately, qualifying widow(er), or head of household. The IRS updates these amounts annually, reflecting inflation and economic adjustments. Always consult the latest IRS publications for the current year's figures. Failure to do so could lead to an inaccurate calculation and potential penalties. Furthermore, your age also influences your standard deduction. Individuals age 65 or older, and those who are blind, receive an additional deduction, increasing the overall amount they can subtract.

Determining your filing status is crucial; this single decision significantly impacts your standard deduction amount. For example, married couples filing jointly generally receive a larger standard deduction than those filing separately. If you're unsure about your correct filing status, review the IRS guidelines or consult a tax professional. They can guide you through the intricacies of different statuses and their effects on your taxes. Remember, choosing the wrong status can lead to a miscalculated tax and possible penalties; accurate determination is paramount. Don't hesitate to seek assistance; tax professionals offer invaluable expertise. This precise knowledge ensures you're correctly utilizing the system designed for taxpayer benefit.

Your adjusted gross income (AGI) doesn't directly affect your standard deduction calculation, but it indirectly influences whether itemizing is advantageous. If your itemized deductions exceed your standard deduction amount, itemizing reduces your taxable income more effectively. Therefore, even though you calculate the standard deduction independently, your AGI serves as a crucial comparator when deciding between itemizing and taking the standard deduction. Remember, the goal is to minimize your tax liability using the most beneficial method for your unique circumstances. Analyzing both options is paramount to making an informed choice; don't just settle for the simpler method if it's not the most financially beneficial.

Calculating your standard deduction involves adding together your basic deduction and any additional deductions you qualify for. The basic deduction varies based on your filing status and is publicly available from the IRS website. For additional deductions, review your circumstances carefully to determine eligibility. These include extra deductions for those aged 65 or older or for those who are blind. These additions to the standard deduction can significantly impact your final tax liability, potentially representing a considerable reduction in your overall taxes. Be aware; some taxpayers may qualify for both additional deductions, further reducing their taxable income.

Several resources are available to help with this calculation. IRS publications provide clear instructions and examples. Tax software programs automate the process, eliminating the possibility of manual calculation errors. Remember, accuracy is key. A minor mistake can have significant consequences, especially in the long term. Don't underestimate the importance of obtaining accurate numbers; seeking help from a tax professional is a sound investment if you're unsure about any aspect of the calculation. They can provide expert guidance and ensure that you are maximizing your deductions and minimizing your tax liability. This professional assistance ensures peace of mind and a confident understanding of your tax obligations.

Don't overlook the impact of your filing status on your overall tax liability. This aspect significantly affects the standard deduction and other tax-related computations. Carefully review your situation to ensure you're using the correct filing status. Using the wrong status can lead to penalties and errors on your tax return. Accuracy is vital, and it's always worth confirming your status with an official IRS publication or seeking advice from a tax professional, especially during times of changing family circumstances or major life events that might alter your filing status. By doing so, you're maximizing your chances of accurate tax calculations and minimizing potential liabilities.

Finally, remember the IRS provides ample resources to aid in accurate tax calculation, from online tools and publications to in-person assistance and phone support. Utilizing these resources will help you calculate your deduction correctly. Also, don't hesitate to consult a tax professional; their expertise can provide valuable insight and guidance, ensuring your tax return is accurate and beneficial. They can answer specific questions and handle complex scenarios, providing peace of mind and helping you avoid costly errors. This proactive approach to tax preparation is an investment in your financial future, allowing you to confidently navigate the intricacies of tax law. Remember, a well-informed taxpayer is a well-protected taxpayer.

4 Tax Credits Unveiled

The Child Tax Credit (CTC) can significantly reduce your tax bill if you have qualifying children. It's a credit, meaning it directly reduces the amount of tax you owe, unlike deductions which reduce your taxable income. To claim the CTC, your child must be under 17 at the end of the tax year, be claimed as a dependent, and be a US citizen, national, or resident alien. There are also income limits, so be sure to check the current IRS guidelines to see if you qualify. The credit amount depends on your adjusted gross income (AGI), and may be partially refundable, meaning you could receive some of the credit back even if you don't owe any taxes. Remember to keep accurate records of your children's information, as you'll need this to file your taxes. Don't hesitate to consult a tax professional if you have any questions.

Next, let's look at the Earned Income Tax Credit (EITC). This credit is designed to help low-to-moderate-income working individuals and families. Eligibility is based on your income, filing status, and the number of qualifying children. Unlike the CTC, the EITC is fully refundable, meaning you can receive the entire credit back even if you don't owe any taxes. This makes the EITC particularly beneficial for low-income taxpayers. The EITC calculation can be complex, involving multiple factors and thresholds, therefore, using tax preparation software or consulting a tax professional is highly recommended to ensure accuracy. The EITC is a valuable tool for families struggling to make ends meet and it's crucial to accurately determine eligibility to maximize its benefits.

Many overlook education credits, yet they offer significant potential savings for students and their families. The American Opportunity Tax Credit (AOTC) and the Lifetime Learning Credit (LLC) help offset the cost of higher education expenses. The AOTC is a credit for the first four years of college, while the LLC can be used for an unlimited number of years. Both credits have income limitations and maximum credit amounts. Make sure to keep all your education-related receipts—tuition bills, student loan statements—as proof of payment for your tax return. Careful planning and understanding of the requirements for these credits can significantly ease the financial burden of higher education. Planning for these credits well in advance is highly recommended to effectively utilize this valuable tax incentive.

For those diligently saving for retirement, the Retirement Savings Contributions Credit (Saver's Credit) provides a valuable incentive. This credit is for taxpayers with modest incomes who contribute to a retirement account, such as a traditional IRA or a 401(k). The credit amount depends on your adjusted gross income (AGI) and the amount you contribute. The credit can

reduce your tax liability, making saving for retirement more accessible. Remember, contributing to retirement accounts offers both tax advantages and future financial security, so taking advantage of the Saver's Credit enhances those benefits. Remember to always consult your financial advisor and review current IRS guidelines to confirm your eligibility for the Saver's Credit.
Beyond the major credits, several other valuable tax credits exist. These credits often target specific circumstances or demographics. Researching the options relevant to your situation—whether it's the child and dependent care credit, the adoption tax credit, or other lesser-known credits—can uncover substantial savings. The IRS website provides a comprehensive list of all available credits, along with detailed explanations of eligibility requirements and claiming procedures. The key to maximizing your tax benefits is thorough research and staying updated on the most current tax laws. Don't be afraid to seek professional advice to navigate these complexities and unlock all possible tax credits for your unique circumstances. By carefully investigating available options and properly documenting expenses, you can realize meaningful tax savings.

4.1 Child Tax Credit

The Child Tax Credit (CTC) can significantly reduce your tax liability, offering substantial financial relief to families. It's a credit, meaning it directly reduces the amount of tax you owe, unlike deductions which reduce your taxable income. To claim it, you'll need to meet specific requirements and gather necessary documentation. The key is preparation; a little upfront effort can save you considerable money come tax season.

Understanding the CTC begins with qualifying children. Each child must meet several tests: relationship, age, residency, and joint return. They must be your son, daughter, stepchild, foster child, sibling, stepsibling, or a descendant of any of these. Generally, they must be under age 17 at the end of the year and be claimed as a dependent on your tax return. They must also live with you in the U.S. for over half the year, and not file a joint return unless only to claim a refund. These rules aren't universally applicable, and nuances exist that you must pay attention to.

The credit amount itself depends on your child's age and your adjusted gross income (AGI). For 2023, the maximum credit per qualifying child is $2,000. For children under age 6, there's an additional $600 credit; that means a potential total of $2,600 for younger children. However, the full amount isn't always available. The credit starts to phase out for higher incomes. For example, the refundable part of the CTC may begin to be reduced if your AGI exceeds a specific threshold; check the current IRS guidelines for precise details on phase-out limits, as these amounts change yearly. Failure to properly document the age of each child claimed may delay your refund.

Beyond the basic requirements, there are certain situations that require careful consideration. For instance, if you share custody of your child, there are specific rules determining who can claim the child and receive the credit. Generally, the parent with whom the child lived for the longer part of the year is entitled to the credit, which can be complex in a high conflict situation. It's advisable to carefully review the guidelines if you are in this situation or seek professional advice, if necessary, to avoid potential penalties or disputes.

Remember, claiming the CTC requires accuracy and meticulous record-keeping. You need to gather documentation proving your children's ages, your filing status, and your income level. This may include birth certificates, social security numbers, and W-2 forms. The IRS closely scrutinizes CTC claims, so errors can lead to delays or even rejection of your claim. Therefore, double-checking your paperwork and ensuring that all information is correct is essential.

Navigating the intricacies of the CTC can be challenging, particularly for first-time filers. Utilizing tax preparation software or consulting with a tax professional can provide invaluable assistance. These resources can help you determine your eligibility, accurately calculate your credit amount, and ensure your return is properly filed. Don't underestimate the value of professional help, especially if your situation is complicated or you lack confidence in handling tax matters independently.

Furthermore, it's beneficial to understand the difference between the refundable and non-refundable portions of the CTC. The refundable part can reduce your tax liability to zero and result in a refund. Conversely, the non-refundable part only reduces your tax liability to zero and won't generate a refund. Knowing this distinction is key to understanding the maximum potential benefit you can receive. Plan accordingly by carefully considering how to maximize your refund by understanding what impacts this section of the credit.

Tax laws are complex and subject to change. Staying informed about updates and recent legislation is crucial. The IRS website offers a wealth of resources, including publications and FAQs, to help you understand the rules and requirements. Take advantage of these resources to ensure compliance and maximize your eligibility for the credit. Regularly reviewing the current IRS guidelines to ensure compliance and maximize your potential benefits is important.

In conclusion, the Child Tax Credit offers significant financial relief to families. By understanding the eligibility requirements, carefully gathering necessary documentation, and using available resources such as tax software or professional tax preparation, you can navigate the complexities of the CTC and maximize your savings. Remember that accuracy and careful attention to detail are crucial in maximizing your benefits and avoiding potential issues with the IRS. It's an important credit, worth the effort to learn and claim correctly.

4.2 Earned Income Tax Credit

The Earned Income Tax Credit (EITC) offers a significant tax break to low-to-moderate-income working individuals and families. It's a refundable credit, meaning you can receive a refund even if your credit exceeds your tax liability. Unlike many other credits, the EITC doesn't require you to itemize your deductions; it's available to those who file using the standard deduction as well. This makes it incredibly accessible and beneficial for a large segment of the population. Understanding the nuances of the EITC, however, is crucial to maximizing its benefits. Eligibility requirements change annually, so always refer to the most up-to-date IRS guidelines.

Many people mistakenly believe the EITC is only for those with children. While having qualifying children significantly increases the credit amount, single individuals and couples without children can also qualify, although the amount will generally be lower. Your eligibility depends on factors like your adjusted gross income (AGI), filing status, and the number of qualifying children you have. Crucially, the AGI limit changes annually, so you must carefully review the current IRS guidelines.

To qualify for the EITC, you must meet several requirements. For example, you must be a U.S. citizen or resident alien, and you must have earned income. This income typically consists of wages, salaries, tips, and other compensation received for work. Self-employment income also qualifies, provided you meet the criteria. Investment income, such as interest and dividends, is generally not considered earned income for this purpose. Be aware that there are limits placed on how much investment income you can have and still qualify; exceeding this limit disqualifies you from the credit.

The amount of the EITC you can claim depends on your adjusted gross income (AGI), your filing status (single, married filing jointly, etc.), and the number of qualifying children you have. The more children you have, and the lower your income, the larger your potential credit. For the most accurate calculation, you should use the official IRS EITC Assistant tool or consult a qualified tax professional. These tools will walk you through the process step by step, asking you all the necessary questions to determine your eligibility and your potential refund.

Filing your taxes accurately is vital to receiving the full EITC amount. Errors in reporting your income or family situation can lead to delays or denial of the credit. Keep all your relevant tax documents, such as your W-2s and 1099s, organized and readily accessible during tax season. Carefully review all information provided on your tax return to ensure accuracy before filing. If you are unsure about any aspect of the process, seeking help from a tax professional can save you time, stress, and potential financial loss.

Preparing for tax season ahead of time significantly streamlines the process. Gather your financial records well in advance of the filing deadline to avoid last-minute stress. Organize your documents by category – income, expenses, deductions, credits – for easy access. The IRS website offers helpful resources and tools, including publications that explain the various tax credits and deductions in detail. Familiarizing yourself with this information early can greatly simplify the tax preparation process, allowing you to focus on ensuring the accuracy of your filing.

Claiming the EITC requires careful attention to detail and a thorough understanding of the requirements. Mistakes can lead to delays or even the denial of your credit. Double-checking your information, carefully reviewing all relevant documentation, and seeking assistance from a tax professional if necessary are crucial steps to ensure a smooth and successful filing process. Remember that the IRS provides numerous resources to assist taxpayers, including online tools, publications, and telephone assistance. Take advantage of these resources to navigate the EITC effectively.

In conclusion, the Earned Income Tax Credit provides a significant opportunity for low-to-moderate-income individuals and families to reduce their tax liability. By understanding the eligibility requirements, carefully collecting your tax documents, and accurately completing your tax return, you can maximize your chances of receiving the full amount of the credit you are entitled to. Don't hesitate to utilize the IRS resources and seek professional assistance when needed to ensure a successful filing experience. Proper planning and attention to detail can make a substantial difference in your tax refund. Remember, the EITC is a valuable tool, but it's crucial to use it correctly.

4.3 Education Credits

The American Opportunity Tax Credit (AOTC) and the Lifetime Learning Credit (LLC) are two significant education credits designed to help families finance higher education. The AOTC,

for example, offers a maximum credit of $2,500 per eligible student for the first four years of post-secondary education. This isn't pocket change, representing a substantial reduction in the overall cost of college. Think of it as a significant incentive to pursue further learning. It's a powerful tool for families navigating the often-daunting landscape of higher education expenses.
Eligibility for the AOTC hinges on several factors, including student status (must be pursuing a degree or other credential at an eligible educational institution), enrollment (at least half-time), and modified adjusted gross income (MAGI) limitations. It's crucial to meticulously review these requirements to ensure qualification. Failing to meet even one criterion can disqualify you, resulting in a missed opportunity to claim this valuable credit. Remember, attention to detail is key when dealing with tax regulations.

Conversely, the LLC offers a maximum credit of $2,000 per eligible student, irrespective of the number of years in college. This means ongoing support throughout a student's education journey, offering valuable financial assistance even beyond the first four years. Unlike the AOTC, the LLC doesn't have the same modified adjusted gross income (MAGI) phaseout limitations, widening the pool of potential beneficiaries. This expanded eligibility makes it a powerful tool for many taxpayers.

Many overlook a vital aspect: the interplay between the AOTC and the LLC. You cannot claim both credits for the same student in the same tax year. The IRS prioritizes the AOTC; if you qualify for both, you'll receive the AOTC. This prioritization highlights the importance of understanding the nuances of each credit to maximize your tax benefits. Careful planning and a clear understanding of IRS guidelines are paramount.

Claiming these education credits involves providing specific documentation. This includes Form 1098-T from the educational institution, detailing tuition and fees paid. Accurate and complete documentation is essential for a smooth and successful claim process. Without the necessary documentation, your claim may be delayed, or worse, rejected. Therefore, always retain your tax documents diligently. Keep organized records, a critical practice for many tax-related matters.

Beyond the AOTC and LLC, other tax benefits might apply to educational expenses. For example, you can deduct expenses paid for tuition and other educational expenses from your Adjusted Gross Income (AGI), though the exact rules for deductibility can be complex and may depend on your specific circumstances. Remember, consulting with a tax professional is always an excellent option to ensure compliance. While the guidance here is intended to be helpful, there may be nuances to your personal situation which require professional assistance.

Furthermore, consider state-level education credits or deductions. Many states offer their own tax benefits for higher education, potentially supplementing the federal credits. This emphasizes the importance of researching both federal and state tax laws to fully harness available benefits. Don't overlook state-level benefits – sometimes significant tax relief remains unclaimed simply due to lack of awareness.

Planning for education-related expenses necessitates a long-term perspective. Start saving early to prepare for these substantial costs. Consider strategies such as 529 plans, which offer tax-advantaged savings specifically designed to fund higher education. While this is mentioned elsewhere in this book, it bears repeating the importance of early and consistent planning to reduce the financial strain on families.

The best way to avoid claiming errors and maximize your potential tax savings is by understanding the specific requirements of each credit and keeping detailed records of your education-related expenses. Always double-check the IRS's current guidelines, as tax laws can change annually. Proactive planning and meticulous record-keeping are critical to a successful claim and maximizing potential tax benefits. This helps to ensure a smooth and successful tax-filing experience, allowing you to focus on other priorities. Remember, being informed and organized makes a significant difference.

4.4 Retirement Savings Contributions Credit

The Retirement Savings Contributions Credit (RSCC) offers a valuable opportunity to reduce your tax liability if you contribute to a retirement account. This credit isn't a guaranteed handout; it's designed to incentivize saving for your future, specifically targeting those with modest incomes. Understanding its intricacies is key to maximizing its benefit.

Eligibility hinges on your adjusted gross income (AGI) and the amount you contribute to a qualified retirement account. The AGI limits fluctuate annually, so always consult the most current IRS guidelines. They typically establish a range of AGIs for which you qualify for a partial or full credit. For example, in a given year, a single filer might qualify for the full credit with an AGI below a certain threshold, a partial credit with an AGI above that but below another, and nothing above that point. The crucial point is that there is a credit, but its amount changes according to the income level.

The type of retirement account also matters. The RSCC applies to contributions made to traditional IRAs, Roth IRAs, and employer-sponsored retirement plans like 401(k)s. However, there are important distinctions. For instance, the contribution you make to a Roth IRA will be relevant only if it was made after-tax, therefore this credit is not meant for Roth IRA contributions made via pre-tax deductions. The maximum contribution amount that can qualify for the credit is also capped annually. These limits are adjusted annually and should be consulted on the IRS website.

Calculating the credit involves a multi-step process. First, determine your contribution amount for the tax year. Next, find your modified AGI, since this affects your credit calculation. Then, use your modified AGI to determine your applicable contribution percentage, and finally, your applicable contribution amount. The credit is calculated on the smaller of your contribution or the calculated eligible amount, as defined by the IRS.

This is a crucial detail; the credit is not a simple percentage of your total contribution. It's a percentage of the eligible contribution, an amount that is capped based on your AGI.

Many taxpayers overlook the RSCC because the process seems complex. However, the potential savings can be significant, especially for those working towards retirement while also managing other financial responsibilities. Think of it this way; even a small reduction in your tax bill can translate into a larger sum saved for retirement, effectively boosting your savings over time.

The RSCC isn't simply a tax break; it's a strategic tool for retirement planning. By understanding the requirements and carefully planning your contributions, you can take advantage of this valuable incentive. Consider consulting a tax professional if you're uncertain about your eligibility or how to calculate the credit. They can help you navigate the intricacies and ensure you claim the maximum credit you're entitled to. Don't let the complexities scare you away; the potential benefits outweigh the effort.

Keep accurate records of all your retirement contributions throughout the year. This is essential for filing your taxes accurately and claiming the credit. Gather your contribution statements from your employer-sponsored plan or your IRA provider, and maintain those records systematically, even if you are using a tax software application that does all the calculation for you. The IRS may request this documentation if they audit your return, and having a clear record minimizes the hassle of such an event. Furthermore, maintaining records simplifies the process significantly during tax season. The process of retrieving all the information in due time is time-consuming and stressful.

Remember that tax laws change frequently. The information presented here is intended to provide a general overview. It's vital to consult the official IRS publications and website for the most up-to-date information concerning the RSCC and any other related tax matters before filing your return. The IRS publications contain all the necessary detail, forms, and instructions to accurately and timely file your taxes. Failing to do so could result in penalties or inaccurate refunds.

The RSCC represents a significant opportunity for many taxpayers to enhance their retirement savings. By strategically planning your contributions and carefully understanding the requirements, you can benefit substantially from this valuable credit, supplementing your retirement savings while also lowering your overall tax burden. Don't hesitate to reach out for professional guidance when necessary. This proactive approach to your taxes can provide long-term financial stability. The peace of mind that comes with knowing you have maximized all possible tax advantages is invaluable. So, take the time to understand this often-overlooked credit, and reap the rewards of financially planning ahead.

4.5 Other Notable Credits

The Adoption Tax Credit offers significant financial relief to families welcoming a child into their homes through adoption. This credit helps offset the often substantial costs associated with the adoption process, including legal fees, court costs, and travel expenses. Eligibility requirements generally include being a U.S. citizen or resident alien, having a child placed with you for adoption, and meeting specific income limitations. Importantly, the credit is nonrefundable, meaning it can reduce your tax liability to zero, but you won't receive any of the credit back as a refund. Careful documentation is essential for claiming this credit, so keep detailed records of all adoption-related expenses. Consult a tax professional if you have complex adoption circumstances. Thorough planning beforehand will greatly improve your chances of maximizing this valuable credit.
Unlike many credits focused on income, the Foreign Tax Credit operates within a different realm. It offers relief to taxpayers who have already paid taxes to a foreign country on their income. This avoids double taxation, a critical concern for individuals and businesses with international dealings. To claim the credit, you must meticulously keep records of foreign tax payments and file the necessary forms. The calculation can be complex, often requiring specialized tax software or professional assistance. Understanding the intricacies of foreign tax laws and the intricacies of the credit's limitations is crucial. The amount of the credit is often limited, so careful planning and

potentially professional consultation are key to obtaining the maximum benefit. Careful record-keeping throughout the entire year cannot be stressed enough, particularly when dealing with international finances.

The Premium Tax Credit, significantly impacting healthcare costs, provides substantial assistance for individuals and families purchasing health insurance through the Affordable Care Act (ACA) marketplaces. This credit helps make health insurance more affordable by lowering monthly premiums. Eligibility is determined by income level and the cost of plans available in your area. Many factors influence the amount of the credit, including household income, family size, and the cost of health insurance plans in your marketplace. The credit is generally claimed when filing your annual tax return, but advance payments can often be made monthly to reduce the burden on your monthly budget. It is important to understand how changes in your income and household situation can affect the credit's amount throughout the year.

The Residential Energy Credit incentivizes homeowners to invest in energy-efficient upgrades. This credit, focused on reducing energy consumption and carbon footprints, offers a percentage of the costs incurred for qualified improvements. These improvements include solar electric panels, solar water heaters, and various energy-efficient home upgrades that meet specific energy-saving criteria. The credit itself may be limited to a maximum amount depending on the specific type of improvement and the prevailing rules in place. Claiming the credit requires providing detailed documentation from the installer and proof of payment. Keep those receipts and records organized throughout the renovation process. Planning for such upgrades is an excellent strategy to combine reducing energy costs and benefiting from tax relief. This credit offers a double incentive: lower energy bills and a reduced tax burden.

For those pursuing higher education, several education credits can significantly reduce the financial burden of college. The American Opportunity Tax Credit (AOTC) and the Lifetime Learning Credit (LLC) are among the most notable. The AOTC offers a larger credit but applies only to the first four years of college, while the LLC is for any year of college education. Both credits are nonrefundable, and eligibility depends on factors such as the student's enrollment status, modified adjusted gross income (MAGI), and the cost of education expenses. Detailed record-keeping, including tuition statements and other educational expenses, is paramount for claiming either credit. Properly organizing this documentation will ensure the eligibility requirements are met and the correct amount of the credit is claimed. Careful consideration of both credits and selecting the one best-suited for your individual circumstances is essential to maximizing tax benefits.

5 Tax Planning for Families

The Dependent Care Credit offers significant relief to families with childcare expenses. This credit is designed to help offset the cost of caring for qualifying children or other dependents so that you can work or look for work. To claim it, your dependent must be under age 13 and live with you for more than half the year. The amount of care expenses you can include depends on your adjusted gross income (AGI) and the number of qualifying individuals. Remember, you must itemize to claim this credit; it's not available if you're using the standard deduction. Thorough record-keeping, including receipts and invoices from your childcare provider, is absolutely essential for substantiating your claim and avoiding any potential audits. Don't forget to keep detailed records of your adjusted gross income as well, as this impacts the credit amount significantly. Planning ahead and considering childcare expenses when budgeting can help you prepare for this credit and maximize its benefits. Remember, this credit is a valuable tool for families juggling work and childcare responsibilities.

Education savings plans, particularly 529 plans, offer substantial tax advantages for families saving for their children's future education. These plans allow contributions to grow tax-deferred, meaning you won't pay taxes on the earnings until they are withdrawn for qualified education expenses. This deferral significantly boosts your savings over time. Furthermore, many states offer a deduction or credit for contributions made to their state's 529 plan. This means you'll likely receive additional tax benefits at the state level, which further reduces your overall tax liability. Choosing the right plan involves considering your state's offerings and the potential future educational plans for your children. Remember, funds from 529 plans can be used for a wide range of education-related expenses, including tuition, fees, room and board, and even certain books and supplies. It is always advisable to consult a financial advisor to determine the best approach for your specific circumstances. Proper planning and understanding the rules will help you take full advantage of these tax benefits and ensure a brighter financial future for your children.

Beyond 529 plans, other strategies for tax-efficient saving for education exist. For instance, consider using Coverdell Education Savings Accounts (ESAs). While contribution limits are lower than for 529s, ESAs offer more flexibility regarding the types of expenses you can use the funds for. Always check the current contribution limits and income restrictions. You could explore using a Roth IRA (Retirement Investment Account), but remember this requires a longer-term investment strategy because withdrawals for education before retirement typically incur a 10% early withdrawal penalty unless it applies to higher education expenses, so it's not an immediate solution. You might also explore the American Opportunity Tax Credit and the Lifetime Learning Credit, which can provide substantial immediate tax relief on educational expenses, but remember those are credits that you can claim only once the expense is made, and this is an important factor to consider. This requires careful consideration of current tax laws, and professional tax advice is invaluable for optimal planning.

Family tax planning requires understanding various tax credits and deductions specific to family circumstances. For example, the Child Tax Credit (CTC) provides a direct reduction in your tax liability for each qualifying child. The amount depends on your income and the number of qualifying children. However, the CTC is subject to income limitations, so higher-income families may receive a smaller credit or none at all. It's crucial to understand the phase-out rules to accurately determine your eligibility and the potential credit amount. Keep accurate records of your children's information, Social Security numbers, and dates of birth to ensure a smooth filing process. Remember, changes in tax laws happen, so stay updated on the current regulations for the CTC. Effective planning, which takes into account factors like income and family size, can maximize the benefit of this valuable credit.

Considering your family's total financial situation holistically is key to effective tax planning. Factors such as your income, number of dependents, and other deductible expenses significantly influence the strategies most suitable for your unique situation. Don't just focus on a single credit or deduction, but instead consider how different options interact. For example, choosing between itemizing and using the standard deduction is a crucial decision that can be influenced by several factors, not least the amount of eligible childcare or other deductible expenses. Professional tax advice can be incredibly beneficial in navigating these complex considerations. While online resources and tax software can provide guidance, consulting a tax advisor provides personalized recommendations that account for your specific circumstances and offer a valuable second opinion when making critical financial decisions. Proactive and informed planning, using all available resources, is the best way to safeguard your family's financial future and take full advantage of tax benefits.

5.1 Dependent Care Credit

The Dependent Care Credit offers significant tax relief to families with qualifying childcare expenses. It's designed to help offset the costs of caring for dependents so you can work or look for work. Remember, this isn't a free pass; specific requirements must be met. Eligibility hinges on several key factors, including the age of your dependent and the amount you pay for care.

To claim the credit, your dependent must be under age 13 and either your qualifying child or qualifying relative. The IRS has specific definitions for both. For example, a qualifying child must be claimed as a dependent on your tax return and meet certain residency and support tests. A qualifying relative, on the other hand, is someone you support and who meets other requirements, such as having a gross income under a certain amount. This careful consideration of definitions is crucial for accurately claiming the credit.

The expenses you can include are those paid for the care of your dependent to allow you to work or look for work. This covers a wide range of expenses, from daycare centers and preschools to nannies and babysitters. However, be sure to keep meticulous records of these expenses, including dates, amounts paid, and the name and address of the caregiver. You'll need this documentation to support your claim during an audit. Failing to keep accurate records is a common reason for denial.

The amount of the credit is calculated based on your earned income and the amount of qualifying expenses you paid. It's a nonrefundable credit, meaning it can reduce your tax liability to zero, but you won't receive a refund for any excess credit amount. The calculation can be complex, so using tax software or consulting a tax professional is advisable, particularly if your situation involves multiple dependents or complicated income scenarios.

There are limits to how much you can claim. The credit is limited to the lower of your earned income or the actual expenses paid, further limiting the total credit you can receive. If your situation is complex, involving more than one child, for example, seeking professional help will prevent errors. For example, if you earned $10,000 and paid $5,000 in childcare expenses, the maximum credit you could claim would be $5,000– the maximum amount of qualifying expenses. The calculation becomes less straightforward when you add other factors.

The credit is calculated using a percentage, which varies based on your adjusted gross income (AGI). The higher your AGI, the lower the percentage. The percentage applied to your qualifying expenses directly impacts the credit amount, illustrating the interplay between income and tax benefits. This credit is subject to changes annually, which underscores the need to consult updated tax regulations and guidelines.

While claiming the Dependent Care Credit can significantly reduce your tax burden, it's crucial to understand the specific rules and limitations. There are several common pitfalls to avoid. For example, some expenses may not qualify, such as tuition for school-age children. Likewise, if you are unemployed, you won't be able to claim this tax benefit because you aren't working or searching for work.

Improperly documenting expenses is another prevalent issue. The IRS requires substantial documentation to prove eligibility. Thus, it's advisable to keep detailed records of all your expenses, including receipts and invoices. Accurate and complete record-keeping isn't just for peace of mind; it's a legal requirement. A well-maintained record minimizes the risk of complications during tax season.

Moreover, understanding the difference between a dependent and a qualifying child or relative is critical. The IRS has specific definitions for each, and failure to meet these requirements could result in a denial of your claim. Consulting a tax advisor can clarify any uncertainties related to your specific circumstances.

Finally, keep in mind that the Dependent Care Credit is one tool among many for family tax planning. It's most effective when combined with other strategies, such as education savings plans or retirement account contributions. A holistic approach to family tax planning yields the best results. Remember, careful planning is key to maximizing your tax benefits.

5.2 Education Savings Plans

Saving for your child's education can feel daunting, but understanding the tax advantages available can make the process significantly easier. One powerful tool is the 529 plan, a tax-advantaged savings plan designed specifically for education expenses. Contributions aren't tax-deductible at the federal level, but the earnings grow tax-deferred, meaning you won't pay taxes on the investment growth until you withdraw the funds for qualified education expenses. This deferral allows your savings to compound significantly over time. Moreover, distributions used for tuition, fees, and certain other education-related costs are generally tax-free at the federal level, a significant benefit that reduces your overall tax burden. Remember to check your state's rules; many states offer additional tax benefits, such as state income tax deductions for contributions to their own state's 529 plan. This added layer of tax advantages can considerably boost your savings' growth. Strategic planning, even small contributions over a long period, can make a considerable difference in reaching your education goals.

The beauty of a 529 plan lies in its flexibility. You can choose from various investment options, aligning your risk tolerance with your long-term goals. Some plans offer age-based portfolios, automatically adjusting the investment mix as your child grows older and gets closer to college. This simplifies investment decisions and reduces the need for constant adjustments. Others offer a wider range of individual funds, giving you more control over your investments. However, remember that careful consideration of investment risk is crucial, especially when dealing with long-term savings. While the tax advantages are significant, you want to ensure the investments themselves align with your financial risk tolerance. Understanding your personal risk tolerance and choosing the right investment strategy within your 529 plan is key to successful long-term savings.

Beyond 529 plans, consider other options, such as Coverdell Education Savings Accounts (ESAs). ESAs also offer tax-free growth and withdrawals for qualified education expenses, but they have stricter contribution limits. The annual contribution limit is relatively low, making them more suitable as a supplemental savings tool rather than the primary source of funding. This makes them a good complementary approach to a 529 plan, allowing for a diversified savings strategy. Also, remember that there are income limitations for eligibility for ESAs, so it's essential to check if you meet those requirements before using them. They're not a one-size-fits-all solution and should be considered carefully in conjunction with other savings strategies.

For those who have already accumulated some savings outside of tax-advantaged accounts, strategize using those assets. Consider the tax implications of withdrawing from traditional or Roth IRAs for education expenses. While you may have penalties for early withdrawals, you can compare the tax burden against the tax advantages of using a 529 plan and determine the optimal strategy. Each situation is unique, and a thorough evaluation of your financial circumstances is needed before you make any decision. Consult with a tax professional to weigh the pros and cons and avoid unintentional tax pitfalls. Understanding the different possibilities allows you to maximize your financial resources while minimizing tax liability.

Remember, planning for education costs should begin early. The power of compounding means that even small, regular contributions made early can grow substantially over time. Moreover, starting early allows you to weather any market fluctuations and achieve your savings goal. Consider setting up automatic contributions to your chosen plan to make saving consistent and effortless. This disciplined approach not only simplifies saving but also ensures you remain committed to your long-term financial plan. The sooner you start, the less pressure you will feel later, and the more time your investments have to grow. A long-term outlook is a cornerstone of building strong education savings.

6 Tax Planning for Businesses

Accurate record-keeping is paramount. For sole proprietors, meticulously tracking business income and expenses is crucial for maximizing deductions. Use accounting software or a dedicated notebook; the IRS expects detailed records. Categorize each expense, linking it directly to your business activity. Remember to separate personal and business expenses scrupulously; mixing them can lead to audits and penalties. Maintaining organized records simplifies tax preparation and strengthens your position during any potential IRS scrutiny. Don't underestimate the importance of this seemingly mundane task; it's the bedrock of successful tax planning. This careful approach protects your financial interests and avoids costly mistakes down the line. Remember to consult a tax professional for personalized advice tailored to your specific business structure and circumstances.

Choosing the right business structure is a critical decision with significant tax implications. A sole proprietorship, simple to set up, blends business and personal finances, impacting your tax liability directly. S-corporations and LLCs offer more complex structures, allowing for greater tax efficiency through pass-through taxation. However, these structures require more stringent record-keeping and potentially higher professional fees. The optimal structure depends on your business's size, complexity, and long-term goals. Careful consideration of these factors—alongside consulting with a tax advisor—will ensure you choose the structure that best suits your needs and minimizes your overall tax burden. Do your homework; the right decision now will save you money and headaches in the future.

Understanding business expenses is key to minimizing your tax liability. Many common expenses are deductible, reducing your taxable income. These include office supplies, rent, utilities, advertising, professional fees, and travel expenses. However, the rules surrounding deductibility can be intricate, requiring a clear understanding of IRS regulations. For example, home office deductions require precise documentation, proving that part of your home is exclusively used for business. Similarly, travel expenses must be directly related to business activities, and receipts are necessary to support your claims. Keeping comprehensive records is vital, supporting every deduction. It's advisable to seek professional guidance to ensure accurate reporting and avoid costly mistakes. Don't assume all expenses are deductible; some, such as lavish entertainment, may not qualify.

6.1 Sole Proprietorship Deductions

Many sole proprietors, especially those just starting, overlook valuable deductions that can significantly reduce their tax burden. Understanding these deductions is crucial for maximizing profits and ensuring compliance. Careful record-keeping is paramount; maintain detailed records of all business expenses, receipts, and invoices. This diligent approach will not only simplify tax preparation but also provide a clearer picture of your business's financial health. Remember, accuracy is key to avoiding penalties and audits.

The self-employment tax, a significant expense for sole proprietors, is deductible. Half of the self-employment tax you pay is deductible from your gross income. This deduction reduces your overall tax liability, offering valuable relief. Calculating this accurately requires understanding the specific tax rates and your net earnings from self-employment. Consult the IRS Publication 334 for detailed instructions and examples. This publication offers guidance and clarifies any ambiguities you may encounter. Don't hesitate to seek professional advice if you find yourself struggling with the calculations.

Home office deductions are a frequently overlooked benefit for many sole proprietors. If you use a portion of your home exclusively and regularly for business, you can deduct expenses associated with that space. This deduction can include a portion of your mortgage interest, property taxes, utilities, rent, and even depreciation. However, careful record-keeping is essential; you must meticulously document the percentage of your home used for business. The IRS provides specific guidelines regarding eligible expenses and calculations; ensure your claims comply with these regulations. Misinterpreting these rules can lead to penalties.

Beyond the home office, many other business expenses are deductible. These include costs for supplies, equipment, advertising, travel, and professional services such as accounting and legal fees. Remember, these expenses must be directly related to your business operations to be eligible for deduction. For example, commuting costs are generally not deductible, while travel for business meetings or conferences usually is. Again, thorough record-keeping is your best ally. Organize your expenses by category, making it easier to prepare your tax return.

Vehicle expenses can also be significant, but navigating the deduction rules requires attention to detail. If you use your vehicle for business, you can deduct expenses using either the standard mileage rate or the actual expense method. The standard mileage rate is generally simpler, but the actual expense method may be more beneficial in some situations. Consider factors such as the number of business miles driven, vehicle maintenance costs, depreciation, and insurance before choosing the method that best suits your circumstances. Whichever method you select, maintain meticulous records of your mileage logs.

Health insurance premiums are another considerable expense for many self-employed individuals. The Affordable Care Act (ACA) offers provisions for deducting the full amount of health insurance premiums paid by self-employed individuals. This deduction can provide substantial tax savings, especially for those with higher healthcare costs. Ensure you meet all the eligibility requirements and retain all relevant documentation to support your claim. Remember that careful record-keeping, like always, will help during tax season.

Professional development is an investment in your business's future. The costs associated with attending conferences, workshops, or taking courses related to your profession are generally deductible. These expenses contribute directly to your business's success and qualify as deductible business costs. Keeping receipts and certificates of attendance is essential to support these deductions. Similarly, membership fees in professional organizations can be tax-deductible; always check the IRS guidelines to confirm their eligibility.

Remember that the rules and regulations surrounding tax deductions are complex and subject to change. Consult with a qualified tax professional for personalized advice and to ensure compliance with the latest IRS guidelines. They can help you navigate the complexities of sole proprietorship deductions and develop a comprehensive tax strategy tailored to your specific business needs and circumstances. Proactive tax planning can save you money and reduce your stress during tax season. The information presented here is for general guidance only and does not constitute professional tax advice.

6.2 S-Corp & LLC Tax Strategies

Choosing between an S-corp and an LLC significantly impacts your tax obligations. An LLC, or Limited Liability Company, offers pass-through taxation by default, meaning profits and losses are reported on your personal income tax return. This simplicity is attractive for many small business owners. However, you'll pay self-employment taxes on all your business income, a significant consideration. Careful budgeting and planning are crucial to handle these taxes effectively. Remember to consult with a tax professional to determine the best path for your specific circumstances. They can help you navigate the complexities of your particular business structure and financial profile, maximizing your tax savings.

Unlike an LLC, an S-corp offers a distinct tax advantage: the ability to separate your income as an owner from the business's profits. This means you pay yourself a reasonable salary, subject to both income tax and self-employment tax, but you can reduce your self-employment tax burden on the remaining profits. This strategy is particularly beneficial for higher-earning business owners. It involves meticulous record-keeping to ensure accurate reporting of your salary and profit distribution. Failure to maintain this detail could lead to costly penalties and audits. Careful consideration of your business structure is critical in making a choice that maximizes your potential savings.

The decision of forming either an S-corp or an LLC is not simply a matter of tax savings, but encompasses liability protection. Both entities provide a crucial shield separating your personal assets from business debts. This protection limits your personal liability, preventing creditors from seizing your personal assets if the business encounters financial difficulties. This legal separation is a primary benefit, regardless of the chosen tax structure, and should be weighed alongside the tax implications. Your attorney can provide insight into these aspects, which can be critical to securing your personal financial well-being.

However, converting to an S-corp, while potentially lowering your overall tax liability, also comes with added administrative burden and costs. You'll need to comply with stricter regulatory requirements, including shareholder meetings and meticulous record-keeping. Additionally, legal and accounting fees will likely increase. The administrative costs might eat into your tax savings, making it important to accurately assess these additional expenses against the potential tax benefits. A careful analysis is vital to determine the net benefit of this transition, considering both the direct and indirect expenses involved.

Tax planning for S-corps and LLCs goes beyond simply choosing the right entity. Strategic expense management plays a pivotal role in minimizing your tax liability. Accurately tracking all business expenses and ensuring they are properly categorized is critical for accurate tax reporting. Utilize accounting software to streamline this process and ensure compliance. Proper categorization and documentation allow you to claim all legitimate business deductions, thereby minimizing your taxable income.

This disciplined approach ensures accuracy and reduces the risk of tax audits and associated penalties.

Remember, accurate record-keeping isn't just about claiming deductions; it's about demonstrating your financial position for loans and future investments. Lenders and investors will closely examine your financial statements, relying on precise data to assess risk and viability. Maintaining meticulous records, regardless of the entity chosen, is therefore essential for not only tax compliance but also future business success and growth. This forward-thinking approach safeguards your business's financial health and opportunities.

Moreover, effective tax planning often involves proactive engagement with tax professionals. Consult a CPA or other qualified tax advisor early on in the business creation process. They can advise on the best structure and strategy for your situation, helping to navigate the complexities of tax laws. Regularly consult with your advisor to review your strategy and make adjustments as your business evolves and grows. This consistent interaction ensures your tax plan aligns with your evolving needs and business activities.

Lastly, understanding state tax implications is just as crucial as federal taxation. State laws vary, impacting both the formation and taxation of both S-corps and LLCs. State tax rates and regulations can considerably alter your overall tax burden. Thorough research, ideally conducted in conjunction with a tax professional familiar with state-specific regulations, is necessary to navigate these variations. Understanding these state-level nuances is critical to ensure complete tax compliance and optimize your overall tax strategy.

6.3 Business Expense Tracking

Accurate business expense tracking is crucial for minimizing your tax liability and maximizing deductions. Failing to meticulously document your expenses can lead to missed opportunities for tax savings, potentially resulting in a significantly higher tax bill. This is especially true for self-employed individuals and small business owners, who often face more complex tax situations compared to employees. Therefore, establishing a robust system from the outset is paramount.

The first step involves choosing an appropriate method for tracking expenses. Some prefer using a simple spreadsheet, while others might opt for dedicated accounting software, mobile apps, or even a combination of tools. The best approach depends on your business's size and complexity. A sole proprietor with minimal expenses might find a spreadsheet sufficient, but a larger business would likely benefit from more sophisticated software that provides features like automated expense categorization and reporting. Consider the ease of use, features, and cost-effectiveness when making your selection.

Regardless of the method chosen, consistency is key. Make it a habit to record every business expense immediately, whether it's a purchase receipt, mileage log entry, or a payment made online. Don't rely on memory; details fade and inaccurate recollections can significantly impact your tax return. Keep all receipts, invoices, and other supporting documentation carefully organized. A well-organized filing system, whether physical or digital, will streamline the process during tax season, helping you locate necessary records quickly and efficiently.

It's not just about recording expenses, but also correctly categorizing them. Different expense categories qualify for different tax treatments. For instance, some expenses might be fully deductible, while others may be subject to limitations or require specific substantiation. Understanding the nuances of these categories is essential. For example, you need to differentiate between ordinary and necessary business expenses, which are deductible, and personal expenses, which are not. Familiarize yourself with IRS guidelines, or consult with a tax professional for clarity on specific expense categories relevant to your business.

Remember to separate personal and business expenses meticulously. Mixing personal and business funds can create complexities during tax preparation and increase the risk of IRS scrutiny. Maintain separate bank accounts and credit cards for business transactions whenever possible. This simplifies the process of identifying and tracking legitimate business expenses, reducing the chance of inadvertently claiming personal expenses as business deductions. This not only protects you from potential audits but also ensures the accuracy of your tax filings.

Furthermore, consider utilizing digital tools to your advantage. Many accounting software programs offer features like automatic bank reconciliation and expense categorization, substantially reducing the manual effort involved in tracking expenses. They also typically generate reports tailored for tax preparation, streamlining the process of compiling the necessary information. These tools can help automate routine tasks, freeing up your time to focus on other aspects of your business.

Accurate expense tracking is not merely a tax compliance requirement; it's a critical component of effective financial management. By regularly monitoring your expenses, you gain valuable insights into your business's profitability and cash flow. This information empowers you to make informed decisions about pricing, resource allocation, and cost-cutting measures. Tracking your expenses allows you to identify areas of potential savings and improve your overall financial health. This is a crucial step for any successful business, regardless of its size.

Finally, remember to consult with a tax professional if you have questions or uncertainties about specific expense categories or tax regulations. They can offer personalized guidance tailored to your business structure and financial situation. Don't hesitate to seek professional help; navigating tax laws can be intricate, and expert advice can prove invaluable in ensuring accurate tax reporting and maximizing deductions. It's better to seek clarity and avoid potential penalties than to attempt to navigate the complexities alone. Your tax professional is a valuable ally in this endeavor.

7 Advanced Tax Strategies

Tax loss harvesting allows you to strategically sell losing investments to offset capital gains, reducing your overall tax liability. Imagine you've had a successful year in the stock market, realizing substantial capital gains. However, you also have some investments that have underperformed. Instead of holding onto these losers, you can sell them before the year ends. The resulting capital loss can then be used to offset the gains, lowering your taxable income and, ultimately, your tax bill. This isn't about avoiding paying taxes entirely; it's a smart way to manage your tax obligations more effectively. Remember to meticulously document all transactions, keeping detailed records of purchase and sale prices for every asset. This diligent recordkeeping isn't just good practice; it's crucial for auditing purposes and ensuring you're accurately reporting your capital gains and losses. Consider consulting a tax professional to ensure you fully understand the rules and regulations surrounding tax loss harvesting, as it can become complicated, especially with more complex investment portfolios. They can guide you through the complexities and help you to avoid any unintentional mistakes. Gifting strategies offer a powerful way to transfer wealth while potentially minimizing estate taxes. The annual gift tax exclusion allows you to gift a certain amount of money to each recipient without incurring any gift tax. This amount changes annually, so keeping abreast of the current limits is essential. By making gifts within this exclusion limit, you can reduce your taxable estate, thereby reducing the potential estate tax burden on your heirs. Strategic gifting isn't just about avoiding taxes; it's about thoughtfully planning for the future, ensuring your assets are distributed according to your wishes and minimizing the financial strain on your loved ones after your passing. However, it's important to consult with an estate planning attorney or a qualified financial advisor. They can help you navigate the complexities of gift tax laws and ensure that your gifting strategy aligns with your overall financial and estate planning goals. Failing to do so can lead to unforeseen tax consequences.

Estate tax planning is a crucial element of long-term financial strategy, especially for high-net-worth individuals. Understanding the intricacies of estate tax laws is vital to minimizing the tax burden on your heirs after your death. Several strategies exist, including creating trusts, which can offer significant tax advantages and provide control over the distribution of your assets. Furthermore, life insurance policies can also play a key role. Proceeds from a life insurance policy generally aren't subject to estate tax, offering a way to transfer wealth tax-free to your beneficiaries. It's important to remember that estate planning is not a one-size-fits-all endeavor. Each individual's circumstances are unique, necessitating a personalized approach. Consulting with an estate planning attorney is not simply advisable; it is highly recommended. They will guide you through the best path for your specific situation, taking into account all your assets, liabilities and family structure to create a customized strategy. Failing to plan for your estate can leave your family facing unexpected and possibly devastating financial burdens. Proactive estate planning protects your legacy and ensures your wishes are honored.

7.1 Tax Loss Harvesting

Tax loss harvesting, at its core, is a smart strategy that lets you offset capital gains with capital losses. Imagine you sold a stock for a profit—that's a capital gain, and Uncle Sam wants his share. But, what if you also had investments that lost value? You can use those losses to reduce the taxes you owe on your gains. It's like a financial game of Tetris, fitting losses into the spaces of your gains to create a smaller tax bill. This isn't about avoiding paying taxes altogether; it's about strategically minimizing your tax burden legally and effectively. The beauty of this strategy lies in its ability to transform what might seem like a negative - an investment loss - into a positive: a lower tax bill.

The process is surprisingly straightforward. First, you need to identify investments that have decreased in value. These are your potential loss candidates. It's crucial to carefully track your investment portfolio, noting the purchase price and the current market value. Software designed for investment tracking can simplify this process immensely; numerous options exist for both beginners and seasoned investors alike, offering features such as automated reporting and tax optimization tools. Choose one that suits your needs and technical skills to make your record keeping more efficient.

Next, you sell the losing investments. This officially realizes the loss, making it usable for tax purposes. This is where many people hesitate, fearing that they're locking in their losses. However, the tax benefits often outweigh the emotional resistance. Remember, you aren't necessarily selling at the very bottom; you're strategically utilizing a loss to your advantage. Timing is critical here, but patience and a long-term perspective are beneficial.

The amount of loss you can use to offset gains is limited annually. The IRS allows you to deduct up to $3,000 ($1,500 if you are married filing separately) in capital losses against your ordinary income. Any excess loss can be carried forward to future years to offset future gains. This means that even if you have more losses than gains in a single year, you aren't losing out completely; you're preserving those losses for when the opportunity arises. The rules regarding this annual limit can be intricate, so familiarize yourself with the specific guidelines.

Now, here's where it gets really interesting. Let's say you have more losses than gains. Because you can only deduct $3,000 against ordinary income, you can strategically use a different method. Consider reinvesting the proceeds from your sale of loss-making assets immediately into similar assets. This avoids the temptation to simply hold on to the losing investments hoping for a recovery. Remember, the primary goal is to harvest that loss, reducing your taxable income. This approach effectively allows you to maintain a similar investment strategy while also claiming the tax benefit. You're not giving up on the investment category; rather, you are acquiring essentially the same assets at a revised cost basis.

The Wash Sale Rule is an important consideration here. The IRS prevents you from claiming a loss if you repurchase substantially identical securities within 30 days before or after the sale that generated the loss. Understanding this rule is fundamental to using tax loss harvesting effectively. If you are unsure about the definition of "substantially identical," seek professional advice to avoid violating this rule and undermining your efforts.

Tax loss harvesting isn't a one-size-fits-all solution. It's most effective for investors who have a mix of capital gains and losses in their portfolio. It's particularly beneficial when considering assets held in tax-advantaged accounts versus assets held in taxable accounts. For instance, consider the tax implications of harvesting losses in a Roth IRA versus a taxable brokerage account. Understanding the intricacies of these different account types is critical in strategic tax planning.

Before implementing tax loss harvesting, consult with a qualified tax professional. They can help you navigate the complexities of tax laws and determine the best strategy for your individual financial situation. Remember, this strategy works best within a comprehensive tax plan, considering your overall financial picture. Don't view it in isolation. It is part of a more extensive effort to minimize your total tax liabilities. A financial advisor or tax attorney can help you evaluate your portfolio's position and guide you in achieving the best outcome.

7.2 Gifting Strategies

Gifting, while seemingly simple, offers significant tax advantages when strategically planned. Understanding the annual gift tax exclusion, currently set at a substantial amount, is paramount. This allows you to gift assets, up to this limit, to others each year without incurring gift tax. This isn't just about avoiding taxes; it's about strategically transferring wealth while minimizing future tax burdens for both you and your beneficiaries. Careful consideration of the recipient's financial situation is equally critical. Gifting appreciated assets to those in lower tax brackets allows them to sell those assets and pay taxes at their lower rate, potentially generating significant savings compared to you selling them.

Consider the implications of gifting appreciated assets versus cash. Gifting appreciated assets, like stocks or real estate, shifts the tax burden to the recipient. However, you must carefully weigh the potential capital gains tax implications for the recipient against your own potential tax savings if you were to sell the asset yourself. You need to look at the entire picture to make the correct decision. There are considerations that extend beyond immediate financial implications. Family dynamics play a crucial role in the success of your gifting strategy. Ensuring fair and equitable distribution among beneficiaries, aligned with your intentions, prevents potential conflict and misunderstandings in the future. Open communication and clear documentation are essential aspects of this stage.

Furthermore, establishing a trust can be a powerful tool for managing your assets and minimizing estate taxes. Irrevocable trusts, unlike revocable trusts, are beyond your control once established. They offer protection from creditors and ensure that assets are managed according to your specific instructions. The assets are removed from your taxable estate, providing a substantial estate tax advantage. However, it's crucial to consult with an estate planning attorney to determine the most suitable trust type for your individual needs and circumstances. The complexity of trusts and the potential tax implications require skilled legal advice to make sure that this legal approach is correct for your individual needs. This may vary, depending on the size and complexity of your estate and your long-term goals.

Don't underestimate the power of charitable gifting. Donating appreciated assets directly to a qualified charity eliminates capital gains taxes while providing a tax deduction. This strategy not only supports a cause you believe in but also offers immediate tax benefits, allowing you to reduce your overall tax liability. Strategically selecting the right charity and considering the type of asset you donate can amplify this tax benefit. If you're unsure about the best approach, it is important to consult with a tax advisor before making any decisions.

Careful record-keeping is crucial. Maintain meticulous records of all gifts, including dates, amounts, and recipients. This documentation serves as essential evidence should you ever face an audit or need to demonstrate compliance with tax laws. Detailed records, including donation receipts, trust documents, and valuation reports, protect your interests and simplify the process should you ever need to demonstrate compliance with the tax laws, or need to have proof of a particular transaction.

While gifting strategies offer significant tax advantages, they are not without complexities. Understanding gift tax rules, annual exclusion limits, and the potential implications for both the giver and the recipient is crucial to ensure that your planning is not only effective but also compliant with the tax laws. It's important to remember that these laws are complicated, and it's recommended that you seek help from experts to make sure that your strategy is effective and compliant. The complexities of gift tax laws are such that they necessitate seeking advice from qualified professionals. Ignoring these complexities can lead to costly mistakes.

Ultimately, a well-crafted gifting strategy is a cornerstone of comprehensive tax planning. It involves understanding the interplay between gift tax, estate tax, and income tax, thereby carefully considering the recipient's financial situation, legal frameworks, and the long-term implications of your actions. This means combining careful asset selection with thorough documentation and considering the overall goal. Thorough planning and professional guidance are paramount to maximize tax benefits and align your gifting objectives with your long-term financial goals. Remember, consulting with a tax professional is essential to create a personalized strategy that aligns with your specific financial situation and objectives. Don't hesitate to ask questions and clarify your doubts to build a gifting strategy that is suitable for your needs. It's a long term approach which requires careful planning and professional guidance.

7.3 Estate Tax Planning

Estate tax planning is often overlooked until it's too late, yet it's a crucial element of comprehensive financial planning, especially for those with significant assets. Failing to plan effectively can lead to substantial tax burdens on your heirs, diminishing the inheritance they receive. Proactive planning, however, allows you to mitigate these taxes and ensure your legacy is preserved. Remember, estate tax laws are complex and vary, so seeking professional guidance is paramount.

Unlike income taxes, which are levied annually on your earnings, estate tax applies to the value of your assets at the time of your death. This includes everything you own, from real estate and investments to personal possessions. The current

exemption amount is quite high, offering protection to many individuals, but it's vital to understand this amount can fluctuate with legislation. Moreover, exceeding the exemption could lead to significant tax liabilities, making careful planning essential.
One effective strategy is gifting assets during your lifetime. This reduces the size of your taxable estate. However, this requires careful consideration of gift tax implications. Annual gift tax exclusions allow you to gift a certain amount tax-free to each recipient each year, reducing your overall estate's size without incurring immediate gift taxes. Strategic gifting can significantly lower your estate tax burden, benefitting both you and your beneficiaries.
Establishing trusts can be a powerful tool in estate tax planning. Irrevocable trusts, for example, remove assets from your estate, shielding them from estate taxes. However, you lose control over these assets, so choosing the right trust structure is critical. Revocable trusts, on the other hand, offer greater control while still providing some estate tax advantages. The complexity of trust structures demands expert guidance to ensure your choices align perfectly with your goals and circumstances.
Careful asset allocation is another key aspect of estate tax planning. Diversifying your portfolio reduces risk and can improve overall returns, leading to a healthier estate overall. Holding assets that appreciate in value but aren't subject to significant estate taxes can further help in minimizing your tax liability. This requires understanding the tax implications of various asset classes, and an investment strategy that takes the long-term

view.

Life insurance can be incorporated to offset potential estate taxes. A properly structured life insurance policy can provide a tax-free death benefit to your heirs, providing funds to settle estate taxes without depleting other assets. This allows you to protect your legacy and ensure a smoother transition for your loved ones, something often overlooked by many. However, the cost of life insurance policies should also be factored into overall estate planning.

Don't underestimate the importance of meticulous record-keeping. Maintaining accurate records of your assets, debts, and financial transactions is essential for efficient estate tax planning. This simplifies the process for your executors after your death, minimizing the complexities they face, and ensuring the estate is handled swiftly and efficiently. Good record keeping helps in preparing and filing estate tax returns accurately, decreasing the chances of errors.

Finally, remember the importance of regularly reviewing and updating your estate plan. Life circumstances change, necessitating adjustments to reflect your evolving needs and financial situation. Periodic reviews, ideally with the assistance of a tax professional and estate attorney, help ensure your plan remains effective and aligned with your current goals. Avoid procrastinating; your estate plan shouldn't be a static document, instead treat it as a living, breathing document which requires regular updates. A well-planned estate can secure a smoother transition for your loved ones, providing them with peace of mind and financial security.

www.ingramcontent.com/pod-product-compliance
Lightning Source LLC
LaVergne TN
LVHW022020200926
848481LV00007B/2454
* 9 7 9 8 3 4 8 5 9 5 5 9 3 *